LITTLE Winter COOKBOOK

The Family Circle® Promise of Success

Welcome to the world of Confident Cooking, created for you in the
Family Circle® Test Kitchen, where recipes are double-tested by our team
of home economists to achieve a high standard of success.

MURDOCH BOOKS®

Sydney • London • Vancouver • New York

Little Winter Cookbook

In the past, the food of winter was viewed as stodgy and bland. Today, with the variety of fresh ingredients available throughout winter, there is no need for the cuisine of winter to be as dreary and dismal as winter itself.

Roasted Carrot Soup

Preparation time:
  20 minutes
Total cooking time:
  1¹/₂ hours
Serves 6

1 kg (2 lb) carrots,
  roughly chopped
2 onions, cut into
  wedges
3 cloves garlic
¹/₂ teaspoon chopped
  fresh thyme
60 g (2 oz) butter,
  melted
1 bay leaf
4 fresh parsley stalks
1.5 litres chicken stock
1 tablespoon tomato
  paste
4 thin slices pancetta or
  prosciutto, chopped

1 Preheat the oven to moderate 180°C (350°F/Gas 4). Place the carrot, onion, garlic and thyme in a shallow baking dish. Drizzle with the butter and bake for 1 hour, or until the vegetables are tender and lightly browned. Turn the vegetables occasionally during baking.

2 Transfer the contents of the baking dish to a large pan. Tie the bay leaf and parsley stalks together, and add to the pan with the stock and tomato paste. Bring to the boil and simmer for 20 minutes. Cool for 10 minutes. Remove the bay leaf and parsley.

3 Purée the soup in batches in a blender or food processor. Return to a clean pan and reheat gently. Season with salt and pepper. Heat a small pan, add the pancetta and cook over medium heat until crisp. Sprinkle over the soup and serve.

NUTRITION PER SERVE
Protein 3 g; Fat 9 g; Carbohydrate 10 g; Dietary Fibre 6 g; Cholesterol 30 mg; 550 kJ (130 cal)

Roasted Carrot Soup

Vegetable Soup

Preparation time:
  25 minutes
  + overnight soaking
Total cooking time:
  1 hour 5 minutes
Serves 6

1 cup (200 g/6¹/2 oz)
  dried soup mix
2 tablespoons oil
1 large onion, finely
  chopped
1 green capsicum,
  chopped
2 zucchini, sliced
2 celery sticks, sliced
125 g (4 oz) button
  mushrooms, sliced
2 carrots, sliced
1 large potato, chopped
500 g (1 lb) pumpkin,
  chopped
2 litres vegetable stock

1 Soak the soup mix in
water for 8 hours, or
overnight, then drain.
2 Heat the oil in a large
heavy-based pan and
cook the onion over
medium heat for
10 minutes, or until
soft. Add the capsicum,
zucchini, celery and
mushrooms. Stir-fry for
about 5 minutes.
3 Add the carrot,
potato and pumpkin,
and stir to combine.
Pour in the stock and
add the soup mix.
Bring to the boil, then

reduce the heat.
4 Partially cover the
pan and simmer the
soup for about
45 minutes, or until the
vegetables and soup
mix are soft.

NUTRITION PER SERVE
*Protein 4 g; Fat 7 g;
Carbohydrate 10 g; Dietary
Fibre 4 g; Cholesterol
0 mg; 510 kJ (120 cal)*

Smoked Fish Chowder

Preparation time:
  20 minutes
Total cooking time:
  35 minutes
Serves 4–6

500 g (1 lb) smoked
  haddock
1 large potato, diced
1 celery stick, diced
1 onion, finely
  chopped
50 g (1³/4 oz) butter
1 rasher bacon, rind
  removed and finely
  chopped
2 tablespoons plain
  flour
¹/2 teaspoon mustard
  powder
¹/2 teaspoon
  Worcestershire sauce
1 cup (250 ml/8 fl oz)
  milk
¹/2 cup (30 g/1 oz)
  chopped fresh parsley
¹/4 cup (60 ml/2 fl oz)
  cream, optional

1 Put the fish in a
frying pan, cover with
water and bring to the
boil, then reduce the
heat and simmer for
8 minutes, or until the
fish flakes easily. Strain,
reserving the fish stock,
then peel, bone and
flake the fish. Set aside.
2 Put the potato, celery
and onion in a pan
with 1¹/2 cups (375 ml/
12 fl oz) of the reserved
fish stock. Bring to the
boil, reduce the heat
and simmer for
10 minutes, or until the
vegetables are tender.
3 Meanwhile, melt the
butter in a large pan,
add the bacon and
cook, stirring, for
3 minutes. Add the
flour, mustard and
Worcestershire sauce,
and stir until smooth.
Cook for 1 minute.
Remove from the heat
and gradually add the
milk. Stir until smooth.
Return to the heat and
stir for 5 minutes, or
until the mixture boils
and thickens.
4 Stir in the vegetables
and liquid, then add the
parsley and fish.
Simmer over low heat
for 5 minutes, or until
heated through. Stir in
the cream, season with
salt and pepper, and
serve immediately.

NUTRITION PER SERVE (6)
*Protein 25 g; Fat 15 g;
Carbohydrate 10 g; Dietary
Fibre 1 g; Cholesterol
95 mg; 1100 kJ (260 cal)*

*Smoked Fish Chowder (top)
and Vegetable Soup*

Cabbage Soup

Preparation time:
  20 minutes
Total cooking time:
  40 minutes
Serves 4–6

60 g (2 oz) butter
1 large onion, finely
  diced
1/2 small cabbage,
  finely shredded
3 cups (750 ml/24 fl oz)
  beef stock
1 bay leaf
1/3 cup (90 g/3 oz) sour
  cream
1/3 cup (35 g/1 1/4 oz)
  grated Parmesan

1 Melt the butter in a
pan, add the onion and
sauté over low heat for
10 minutes, or until
soft. Add the cabbage
and cook for 5 minutes.
Add the stock and bay
leaf. Bring to the boil,
then reduce the heat,
cover and simmer for
20 minutes.
2 Season the soup with
salt and pepper before
spooning it into serving
bowls. Top with a
spoonful of the sour
cream and sprinkle
with the grated
Parmesan. Serve with
thick slices of fresh
crusty bread.

NUTRITION PER SERVE (6)
*Protein 4 g; Fat 15 g;
Carbohydrate 2 g; Dietary
Fibre 0 g; Cholesterol
50 mg; 690 kJ (170 cal)*

Curried Parsnip and Potato Soup

Preparation time:
  25 minutes
Total cooking time:
  45 minutes
Serves 4

2 tablespoons oil
1 large onion, chopped
3 teaspoons curry
  powder
1 teaspoon ground
  cumin
1/2 teaspoon ground
  fenugreek
750 g (1 1/2 lb)
  potatoes, cubed
300 g (10 oz) parsnip,
  chopped
1 red apple, unpeeled,
  chopped
1.5 litres vegetable
  stock
1 cup (250 ml/8 fl oz)
  cream
oil, for shallow-frying
3 thick slices white
  bread, crusts
  removed, cubed

1 Heat the oil in a large
heavy-based pan over
low heat. Add the
onion and cook for
10 minutes, or until
golden brown, stirring
occasionally. Add the
curry powder, cumin
and fenugreek, and
cook for 2 minutes.
2 Add the chopped
potato, parsnip and
apple, and cook for
10 minutes, or until
the vegetables begin to
turn golden brown,
tossing regularly.
Slowly stir in 1 cup
(250 ml/8 fl oz) of the
stock, scraping the
bottom of the pan to
remove any sediment.
3 Add the remaining
stock, still stirring to
remove the sediment
from the pan. Cover
and simmer for
10 minutes. Add the
cream and simmer,
uncovered, for
3 minutes. Season well
with salt and black
pepper. Using a potato
masher or fork, mash
some of the large pieces
of vegetable so the soup
is slightly chunky.
Cover and keep warm.
4 Heat the oil in a
frying pan over
medium heat. Add the
bread and cook until
golden brown, turning
the cubes in the oil.
Remove and drain well
on paper towels. Serve
the soup sprinkled with
the croutons.

NUTRITION PER SERVE
*Protein 10 g; Fat 40 g;
Carbohydrate 50 g; Dietary
Fibre 7 g; Cholesterol
85 mg; 2590 kJ (620 cal)*

Note: This is a thick,
hearty soup, but may
be thinned down with a
little water or stock.

*Curried Parsnip and Potato Soup (top)
with Cabbage Soup*

Italian Sausages with Tagliatelle

Preparation time:
 35 minutes
Total cooking time:
 50 minutes
Serves 4–6

2 red capsicums
2 teaspoons olive oil
500 g (1 lb) Italian
 sausages
500 g (1 lb) tagliatelle
1 large onion, sliced
3 cloves garlic, crushed
2 red chillies, chopped
500 g (1 lb) tomatoes,
 roughly chopped
1/4 cup (60 ml/2 fl oz)
 red wine
1 tablespoon balsamic
 vinegar
1 tablespoon chopped
 fresh oregano
2 tablespoons chopped
 fresh parsley

1 Cut the capsicums into large pieces. Place under a hot grill until the skin blackens and blisters. Cool in a plastic bag, then peel away the skin and cut into thin strips.
2 Heat the oil in a large frying pan and brown the sausages. Remove and cut into pieces.
3 Cook the pasta in boiling salted water for 10 minutes, or until *al dente*. Rinse under hot water, and keep warm.
4 Reheat the frying pan over low heat. Cook the onion, garlic and chilli for 10 minutes, stirring occasionally. Add the capsicum and cook for 3 minutes. Add the tomato, wine and vinegar. Cover and simmer for 5 minutes. Mix in the sausage, herbs, salt and pepper. Serve with the pasta.

NUTRITION PER SERVE (6)
Protein 15 g; Fat 20 g; Carbohydrate 30 g; Dietary Fibre 5 g; Cholesterol 55 mg; 1585 kJ (380 cal)

Sweet Potato Ravioli

Preparation time:
 20 minutes
Total cooking time:
 30 minutes
Serves 4

500 g (1 lb) orange
 sweet potato, chopped
2 teaspoons lemon juice
190 g (6 1/2 oz) butter
1/2 cup (50 g/1 3/4 oz)
 grated Parmesan
1 tablespoon chopped
 fresh chives
1 egg, lightly beaten
250 g (8 oz) packet
 won ton wrappers
2 tablespoons chopped
 fresh sage
2 tablespoons chopped
 walnuts

1 Cook the sweet potato and lemon juice in boiling water for 15 minutes, or until tender. Drain and pat dry with paper towels. Cool for 5 minutes.
2 Process the sweet potato and 30 g (1 oz) of the butter in a food processor until smooth. Add the Parmesan, chives and half the egg. Season with salt and freshly ground pepper. Cool completely.
3 Place 2 teaspoons of the mixture in the centre of half the won ton wrappers. Brush the edges with the remaining egg, then cover with the remaining wrappers. Press the edges firmly to seal. Using a 7 cm (2 3/4 inch) cutter, cut the ravioli into circles.
4 Melt the remaining butter in a pan and cook over low heat until golden brown. Remove from the heat.
5 Cook the ravioli in batches in a large pan of boiling water for 4 minutes. Drain carefully and divide among heated serving plates. Serve the ravioli immediately, drizzled with the butter and sprinkled with the sage and walnuts.

NUTRITION PER SERVE
Protein 15 g; Fat 50 g; Carbohydrate 30 g; Dietary Fibre 3 g; Cholesterol 190 mg; 2490 kJ (595 cal)

Italian Sausages with Tagliatelle (top) and Sweet Potato Ravioli

Roast Root Vegetables

Preparation time:
  20 minutes
Total cooking time:
  50 minutes
Serves 4

4 parsnips
2 carrots
2 small orange sweet
  potatoes
4 beetroots, cut into
  wedges
8 cloves garlic, unpeeled
1/4 cup (60 ml/2 fl oz)
  oil
1 tablespoon honey
1 teaspoon cumin seeds
1/2 teaspoon cracked
  black pepper
1/2 teaspoon rock salt

1 Preheat the oven to moderately hot 200°C (400°F/Gas 6). Cut the parsnips, carrots and sweet potatoes into 10 cm (4 inch) lengths. Place all the vegetables and garlic in a large baking dish, and drizzle with the oil and honey. Sprinkle with the cumin seeds, pepper and salt. Toss to coat.
2 Bake the vegetables for 40–50 minutes, or until they are tender inside and golden brown outside.

NUTRITION PER SERVE
*Protein 7 g; Fat 15 g;
Carbohydrate 55 g; Dietary
Fibre 10 g; Cholesterol
0 mg; 1590 kJ (380 cal)*

Roast Chicken with Rice Stuffing

Preparation time:
  20 minutes + standing
Total cooking time:
  1 hour 40 minutes
Serves 4

1/2 cup (95 g/3 oz) wild
  rice
15 pitted prunes,
  quartered
2 tablespoons port
1/3 cup (45 g/1 1/2 oz)
  hazelnuts
30 g (1 oz) butter
4 spring onions, finely
  chopped
1/2 green apple,
  coarsely grated
1/2 teaspoon grated
  orange rind
1/2 teaspoon ground
  cardamom
1 egg, lightly beaten
1.5 kg (3 lb) chicken
30 g (1 oz) butter,
  extra, melted

1 Place the rice in a pan and add enough boiling water to come 2.5 cm (1 inch) above the rice. Bring to the boil and cook for 10 minutes. Remove from the heat, cover and leave for 1 hour, then drain well.
2 Preheat the oven to moderate 180°C (350°F/Gas 4). Combine the prunes and port in a bowl, cover and set aside.
3 Bake the hazelnuts on a baking tray for 8 minutes. Wrap in a tea towel and rub off the skins. Coarsely chop the hazelnuts.
4 Melt the butter in a pan and add the spring onion. Cook over low heat, stirring, for 2 minutes, or until soft. Remove from the heat and mix in the rice, prunes, port, hazelnuts, apple, orange rind, cardamom and beaten egg. Season with salt and pepper.
5 Wipe the chicken and pat dry with paper towels. Spoon the stuffing into the cavity and close the cavity with a toothpick or skewer. Tie the wings and drumsticks securely in place with kitchen string. Place on a rack in a deep baking dish.
6 Brush the chicken with the extra melted butter and roast for 1 hour 20 minutes, or until browned and tender. Cover loosely with foil and leave in a warm place for 10 minutes. Remove the toothpicks and string before carving.

NUTRITION PER SERVE
*Protein 100 g; Fat 80 g;
Carbohydrate 40 g; Dietary
Fibre 4 g; Cholesterol
400 mg; 5620 kJ (1340 cal)*

*Roast Chicken with Rice Stuffing (top)
and Roast Root Vegetables*

Beef and Barley Casserole

Preparation time:
  20 minutes
Total cooking time:
  2 hours
Serves 4–6

750 g (1¹/2 lb) chuck
  steak
2 tablespoons oil
2 onions, chopped
2 cloves garlic, crushed
2 teaspoons grated
  fresh ginger
3 cups (750 ml/24 fl oz)
  beef stock
1 cinnamon stick
¹/2 cup (110 g/3¹/2 oz)
  pearl barley
500 g (1 lb) orange
  sweet potato, cut into
  large chunks

1 Trim the steak of any excess fat and sinew, and cut into 2 cm (³/4 inch) cubes. Heat the oil in a large pan and brown the meat in batches, then set aside.
2 Add the onion to the pan and cook for 10 minutes, or until very soft and golden brown, stirring occasionally. Add the garlic and ginger, and cook for 1 minute.
3 Return the meat to the pan with the stock and cinnamon stick. Bring just to the boil, reduce the heat and simmer, covered, for 1 hour. Add the barley and cook for a further 20 minutes.
4 Add the sweet potato and cook, uncovered, for 20 minutes, or until the sweet potato is tender. Stir occasionally so that the sweet potato cooks evenly. Remove the cinnamon stick. Serve with steamed green vegetables.

NUTRITION PER SERVE (6)
*Protein 30 g; Fat 10 g;
Carbohydrate 30 g; Dietary
Fibre 4 g; Cholesterol
85 mg; 1350 kJ (320 cal)*

Macaroni with Cheese Sauce

Preparation time:
  15 minutes
Total cooking time:
  40 minutes
Serves 4

200 g (6¹/2 oz)
  macaroni
60 g (2 oz) butter
1 onion, chopped
2 rashers bacon,
  chopped
¹/4 cup (30 g/1 oz)
  plain flour
2¹/2 cups (600 ml/
  20 fl oz) milk
¹/2 teaspoon ground
  nutmeg
1¹/2 cups (185 g/6 oz)
  grated Cheddar

1 Preheat the oven to moderate 180°C (350°F/Gas 4). Grease a 1.5 litre ovenproof dish. Cook the macaroni in a large pan of rapidly boiling water until tender, then drain.
2 Heat the butter in a large pan and add the onion and bacon. Stir over medium heat for 4 minutes, or until soft. Add the flour and stir over low heat for 1 minute. Remove from the heat and gradually add the milk. Stir until smooth. Return to medium heat and cook, stirring, for 4 minutes, or until the mixture boils and thickens. Simmer over low heat for 1 minute. Remove from the heat and stir in the nutmeg.
3 Add the pasta and two thirds of the cheese. Stir until combined, then spoon into the dish. Sprinkle with the remaining cheese and bake for 20 minutes, or until lightly golden.

NUTRITION PER SERVE
*Protein 25 g; Fat 35 g;
Carbohydrate 30 g; Dietary
Fibre 2 g; Cholesterol
115 mg; 2150 kJ (515 cal)*

Note: To flavour the milk, bring to the boil with 6 peppercorns, a slice of onion and a bay leaf. Remove from the heat, cover and leave for 15 minutes, then strain and use as above.

---

*Macaroni with Cheese Sauce (top)
and Beef and Barley Casserole*

Rabbit Fricassee

Preparation time:
  30 minutes
  + overnight standing
Total cooking time:
  2³/4 hours
Serves 4–6

2 x 750 g (1¹/2 lb)
  rabbits, each cut into
  6 even pieces
2–3 tablespoons white
  vinegar
2 onions, sliced
2 bay leaves
6 cloves
6 black peppercorns
1 celery stick, including
  the leaves
80 g (2³/4 oz) butter
1 onion, thinly sliced
125 g (4 oz) button
  mushrooms, halved
3 rashers bacon,
  chopped
¹/3 cup (40 g/1¹/4 oz)
  plain flour
¹/2 cup (125 ml/4 fl oz)
  cream
¹/3 cup (20 g/³/4 oz)
  chopped fresh parsley

1 Trim any excess fat and sinew from the rabbit and clean under cold water. Place in a large glass or ceramic bowl, cover with water and add 1 tablespoon of vinegar. Cover and refrigerate for several hours or overnight, changing the water and vinegar 2–3 times.
2 Drain the rabbit pieces and put them in a large heavy-based pan. Add the onion, bay leaves, cloves, peppercorns and celery. Cover with water and simmer, covered, over low heat for 2¹/2 hours, or until the meat comes away from the bone. Remove the meat, cover and keep warm. Strain and reserve 2¹/2 cups (600 ml/20 fl oz) of the cooking liquid.
3 Meanwhile, heat 30 g (1 oz) of the butter in a pan. Add the thinly sliced onion, button mushrooms and bacon. Stir for 5 minutes, or until cooked. Set aside.
4 Melt the remaining butter in a large pan. Add the flour and stir for 1 minute. Remove from the heat and whisk in the reserved cooking liquid until smooth. Return to the heat and whisk until the sauce is thick, then cook over medium heat for 2 minutes. Stir in the cream and chopped parsley. Add the bacon mixture and stir for 2–3 minutes, or until heated through. Season with salt and ground black pepper. Add the rabbit pieces and stir gently for 5 minutes to coat the rabbit pieces in the sauce and to heat them through.

NUTRITION PER SERVE (6)
Protein 65 g; Fat 30 g; Carbohydrate 9 g; Dietary Fibre 2 g; Cholesterol 225 mg; 2350 kJ (560 cal)

Rabbit Fricassee

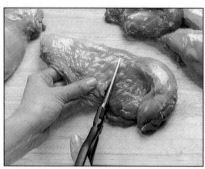

Using a pair of kitchen scissors, cut the rabbits into 6 even pieces.

Once the rabbit is cooked, remove the pieces from the pan.

Melt the butter and stir the onion, mushrooms and bacon until cooked.

Whisk the sauce over the heat until it is thick.

Pork Ribs with Borlotti Beans

Preparation time:
25 minutes
Total cooking time:
1¹/2 hours
Serves 4

200 g (6¹/2 oz) dried
borlotti beans
1 tablespoon olive oil
500 g (1 lb) pork
spareribs, cut into
5 cm (2 inch) pieces
(ask the butcher to do
this)
2 onions, chopped
2 cloves garlic, finely
chopped
2 cups (500 ml/16 fl oz)
chicken stock
2 cups (500 g/1 lb)
tomato pasta sauce
1 teaspoon brown sugar
2 bay leaves
2 large carrots, chopped
1 potato, chopped
1 tablespoon chopped
fresh parsley

1 Cook the borlotti beans in boiling water for 30–40 minutes, or until tender. Drain.
2 Heat the oil in a large deep frying pan, add the spareribs and brown over high heat. Add the onion and garlic. Cook, stirring regularly, for 5 minutes, or until the onion is soft and golden.

3 Add the stock, pasta sauce, sugar and bay leaves. Bring to the boil, then simmer, covered, for 10 minutes. Add the beans, carrot and potato. Season with salt and pepper. Cover, bring to the boil and simmer for 15 minutes, stirring often. Discard the bay leaves. Stir in the parsley.

NUTRITION PER SERVE
Protein 35 g; Fat 50 g;
Carbohydrate 55 g; Dietary
Fibre 10 g; Cholesterol
135 mg; 2340 kJ (775 cal)

Seafood Pie

Preparation time:
25 minutes
Total cooking time:
1 hour
Serves 4

650 g (1 lb 5 oz)
Desiree potatoes
1/2 cup (125 ml/4 fl oz)
white wine
300 ml (10 fl oz) fish
stock or water
750 g (1¹/2 lb) boneless
white fish, cut into
5 cm (2 inch) pieces
50 g (1³/4 oz) butter
1/3 cup (40 g/1¹/4 oz)
plain flour
1/4 cup (60 ml/2 fl oz)
cream
3 gherkins, chopped
1/4 cup (15 g/¹/2 oz)
chopped fresh parsley

12 raw prawns, peeled
and deveined
125 g (4 oz) scallops,
cleaned
1/2 cup (60 g/2 oz)
grated Cheddar

1 Cut the potatoes in half, leaving the skin on. Cook in a pan of boiling salted water for 15 minutes, or until tender. Drain and cool.
2 Meanwhile, heat the wine and fish stock in a pan. Add the fish and simmer for 5 minutes, or until just cooked. Remove the fish and reserve the liquid.
3 Melt the butter in a pan, add the flour and cook for 1 minute. Remove from the heat and gradually add the reserved cooking liquid. Whisk until smooth. Cook over low heat for 2–3 minutes. Stir in the cream, gherkins, parsley and seafood.
4 Preheat the oven to moderate 180°C (350°F/Gas 4). Grease a 2 litre ovenproof dish and spoon in the fish mixture. Peel and grate the potato, season with salt and pepper, and mix well. Spread over the pie and sprinkle with the cheese. Bake for 40 minutes, or until golden brown.

NUTRITION PER SERVE
Protein 45 g; Fat 20 g;
Carbohydrate 30 g; Dietary
Fibre 3 g; Cholesterol
185 mg; 2230 kJ (530 cal)

Pork Ribs with Borlotti Beans (top)
and Seafood Pie

Deep-dish Chicken Pie

Preparation time:
45 minutes + chilling
Total cooking time:
1 hour 10 minutes
Serves 6

2 tablespoons olive oil
1 large onion, chopped
2 cloves garlic, finely
  chopped
600 g (1¹/4 lb) chicken
  thigh fillets, chopped
2 large carrots,
  chopped
2 large parsnips,
  chopped
1 large potato,
  chopped
2 bay leaves
2 celery sticks, thinly
  sliced
¹/4 cup (30 g/1 oz)
  plain flour
1¹/4 cups (315 ml/
  10 fl oz) milk
¹/2 cup (125 ml/4 fl oz)
  chicken stock
3 sheets frozen
  butterpuff pastry,
  thawed (see Note)
1 egg yolk, beaten

1 Heat the oil in a large deep frying pan over medium heat. Cook the onion and garlic for 3 minutes, or until the onion is soft. Add the chopped chicken and cook for 10 minutes, or until golden brown, turning regularly.
2 Add the chopped carrot, parsnip, potato, bay leaves and celery with ¹/4 cup (60 ml/ 2 fl oz) water, and mix well. Cook the mixture over low heat, covered, for 10 minutes, or until the carrot, parsnip and potato are just tender.
3 Stir in the flour and cook for 2 minutes. Remove from the heat and add the milk and stock, stirring constantly until the mixture is blended and smooth. Return to the heat and cook, stirring, until the sauce boils and thickens. Transfer to a large bowl, cover and refrigerate until the chicken mixture is completely cold.
4 Grease the base and side of a deep 20 cm (8 inch) springform tin. Using 1 sheet of the pastry, cut a circle to fit the base of the tin. Press it gently into the tin. Cut the second sheet of pastry into 3 strips and press each strip around the side of the tin, pressing the edges together gently with your fingertips. (Make sure the pastry is well sealed or the filling will leak.) Refrigerate the lined tin for 20 minutes.
5 Preheat the oven to moderately hot 200°C (400°F/Gas 6). Spoon the cold filling into the pastry case and smooth over the top with the back of the spoon. Using the last sheet of pastry, cut a circle 2 cm (³/4 inch) larger than the tin, gently place it over the pie and trim away the excess pastry. Pinch the edges together firmly to seal. Cut a 2 cm (³/4 inch) hole in the centre of the pastry. Decorate the top of the pie with shapes cut out from the excess pastry. Brush the top of the pie with the beaten egg yolk.
6 Bake the pie for 35 minutes, or until it is crisp and golden. Leave in the tin for 10 minutes before removing and cutting into wedges.

NUTRITION PER SERVE
Protein 30 g; Fat 30 g; Carbohydrate 50 g; Dietary Fibre 5 g; Cholesterol 105 mg; 2550 kJ (610 cal)

Note: Butterpuff pastry will produce the best result for this pie. If you can't find butterpuff pastry, buy plain puff pastry and brush it with melted butter. The pastry sheets will take 5–10 minutes to defrost at room temperature. Baking the pie in a springform pan ensures a crisp, firm, golden-brown pastry shell that is easily removed.

Deep-dish Chicken Pie

Winter Fish and Bean Bake

Preparation time:
  10 minutes
Total cooking time:
  45 minutes
Serves 4

1 tablespoon olive oil
1 onion, chopped
1 clove garlic, crushed
50 g (1³/4 oz) thinly
  sliced pancetta,
  chopped
2 zucchini, sliced
1 tablespoon tomato
  paste
425 g (14 oz) can
  crushed tomatoes
1 tablespoon chopped
  fresh marjoram
1 tablespoon chopped
  fresh oregano
310 g (10 oz) can
  canellini beans,
  drained
4 boneless thick white
  fish fillets

1 Preheat the oven to moderate 180°C (350°F/Gas 4). Heat the oil in a large pan and add the onion, garlic and pancetta. Cook until the onion is soft, but not brown. Add the zucchini, tomato paste, tomatoes and herbs.
2 Bring to the boil, reduce the heat and simmer, covered, for 10 minutes. Add the canellini beans. Season with salt and pepper.
3 Place the fish in a single layer in a shallow ovenproof dish. Spoon the sauce over the top. Cover with foil and bake for 25 minutes, or until the fish is cooked. Serve immediately.

NUTRITION PER SERVE
*Protein 20 g; Fat 15 g;
Carbohydrate 6 g; Dietary
Fibre 5 g; Cholesterol
100 mg; 1010 kJ (240 cal)*

Creamy Broccoli and Cheese Soufflé

Preparation time:
  20 minutes
Total cooking time:
  40 minutes
Serves 4

2 tablespoons dry
  breadcrumbs
150 g (5 oz) broccoli,
  cut into florets
45 g (1¹/2 oz) butter
2 tablespoons plain
  flour
1 cup (250 ml/8 fl oz)
  milk
1¹/4 cups (155 g/5 oz)
  grated Cheddar
¹/3 cup (35 g/1¹/4 oz)
  grated Parmesan
4 eggs, at room
  temperature
pinch of ground nutmeg

1 Preheat the oven to moderately hot 190°C (375°F/Gas 5). Grease a 2 litre soufflé dish, then dust with the breadcrumbs. Cook the broccoli in boiling water, partially covered, for 3 minutes, then drain and pat dry. Chop the broccoli roughly.
2 Melt the butter in a large pan. Stir in the flour and cook for 1 minute. Remove from the heat and gradually add the milk. Return to the heat and stir until the mixture thickens. Cook over low heat, stirring, for 1 minute. Remove from the heat and stir in the Cheddar and 3 tablespoons of the Parmesan. Separate the eggs and beat in the egg yolks, one at a time. Season with salt, pepper and nutmeg. Cool slightly, and fold in the broccoli.
3 Beat the egg whites to soft peaks, then stir a third into the sauce. Very gently fold in the remaining egg white with a metal spoon. Pour into the dish and sprinkle with the remaining Parmesan.
4 Bake the soufflé for 30–35 minutes, or until it is well risen and golden. The centre should be creamy and soft. Serve immediately.

NUTRITION PER SERVE
*Protein 25 g; Fat 30 g;
Carbohydrate 10 g; Dietary
Fibre 2 g; Cholesterol
265 mg; 1795 kJ (430 cal)*

*Winter Fish and Bean Bake (top)
with Creamy Broccoli and Cheese Soufflé*

Vegetable Purées

A piping hot vegetable purée is the ideal accompaniment to winter stews and casseroles. These are also an excellent way to serve all of the delicious winter vegetables.

Celeriac and Tarragon Purée

Bring 2 cups (500 ml/16 fl oz) vegetable stock, 2 cups (500 ml/16 fl oz) water and the juice of 1 lemon to the boil. Add 3 peeled and chopped celeriacs, and cook for 10–15 minutes, or until tender. Drain and place in a food processor with 40 g (1¼ oz) butter and 1 tablespoon cream. Season with salt and pepper, and process until smooth. Add 1 tablespoon finely chopped fresh tarragon and process for a further 10 seconds. Serve immediately. Serves 4

NUTRITION PER SERVE
Protein 2 g; Fat 9 g; Carbohydrate 6 g; Dietary Fibre 4 g; Cholesterol 30 mg; 485 kJ (115 cal)

Bashed Neeps

Peel 3 swedes and cut them into eighths. Add to a large pan of boiling water and cook, covered, for 10–15 minutes, or until tender. Drain well and place in a food processor with 40 g (1¼ oz) butter and 1 tablespoon cream. Season with salt and freshly ground black pepper. Process until smooth and serve hot. Serves 4

NUTRITION PER SERVE
Protein 1 g; Fat 10 g; Carbohydrate 3 g; Dietary Fibre 2 g; Cholesterol 30 mg; 440 kJ (105 cal)

Garlic and Onion Purée

Melt 85 g (3 oz) butter in a large heavy-based pan. Add 500 g (1 lb) finely chopped red onions and 6 finely chopped cloves of garlic, and cook over very low heat for 45 minutes, stirring occasionally. Stir in 2 tablespoons balsamic vinegar and 1 teaspoon Dijon mustard, and season with salt and freshly ground black pepper. Cook for a further 10 minutes, stirring to break down the onion mixture. Serve hot. Serves 4

NUTRITION PER SERVE
Protein 3 g; Fat 20 g; Carbohydrate 6 g; Dietary Fibre 3 g; Cholesterol 55 mg; 800 kJ (190 cal)

Turnip and Leek Purée

Cover 6 peeled, quartered turnips with water in a pan. Bring to the boil and add 1 finely sliced leek. Cook for 15 minutes, or until tender. Drain and place in a food processor with 2 tablespoons crème fraîche or sour cream. Season with salt and pepper, and process until smooth. Serve immediately. Serves 4

NUTRITION PER SERVE
Protein 4 g; Fat 4 g; Carbohydrate 10 g; Dietary Fibre 8 g; Cholesterol 15 mg; 390 kJ (95 cal)

Beetroot Purée

Cook 8 peeled and quartered beetroots in a pan of boiling water for 15–20 minutes, or until tender. Drain and place in a food processor with 1/2 teaspoon ground coriander, 1/2 teaspoon ground cumin, 1/4 teaspoon ground cardamom and 2 tablespoons crème fraîche or sour cream. Season to taste. Process until smooth, and serve immediately. Serves 4

NUTRITION PER SERVE
Protein 5 g; Fat 4 g; Carbohydrate 20 g; Dietary Fibre 8 g; Cholesterol 15 mg; 620 kJ (150 cal)

From left: Celeriac and Tarragon Purée; Bashed Neeps; Garlic and Onion Purée; Turnip and Leek Purée; Beetroot Purée

Brussels Sprout Gratin

Preparation time:
  15 minutes
Total cooking time:
  25 minutes
Serves 4

500 g (1 lb) Brussels
  sprouts
60 g (2 oz) butter,
  melted
1 tablespoon oil
1 small onion,
  chopped
2 rashers bacon, finely
  chopped
1/2 cup (40 g/1 1/4 oz)
  fresh breadcrumbs
1 tablespoon chopped
  fresh parsley
1/4 cup (25 g/3/4 oz)
  grated Parmesan

1 Trim the outer leaves from the Brussels sprouts and cut a cross in the stems. Boil or steam for 10 minutes, or until tender. Drain, cut in half and place in an ovenproof dish. Drizzle with the melted butter and toss gently to coat.
2 Heat the oil in a pan, add the chopped onion and cook over medium heat for 5 minutes. Stir in the bacon and cook for 5 minutes. Remove from the heat and place the mixture in a bowl.
3 Combine the breadcrumbs, parsley and 2 tablespoons of the Parmesan with the onion mixture. Season with freshly cracked black pepper. Spoon the breadcrumb mixture over the Brussels sprouts and sprinkle with the remaining Parmesan. Cook under a preheated hot grill for 5 minutes, or until the top is lightly browned. Serve hot.

NUTRITION PER SERVE
*Protein 15 g; Fat 20 g;
Carbohydrate 10 g; Dietary
Fibre 6 g; Cholesterol
55 mg; 1170 kJ (280 cal)*

Herbed Lamb Roast

Preparation time:
  30 minutes
  + 15 minutes standing
Total cooking time:
  1 hour 25 minutes
Serves 4–6

1.5 kg (3 lb) leg of
  lamb
2 cloves garlic, cut into
  quarters
1/4 cup (60 ml/2 fl oz)
  olive oil
2 tablespoons chopped
  fresh rosemary
1 teaspoon salt
1 teaspoon freshly
  ground black pepper
500 g (1 lb) Roma
  tomatoes, halved
500 g (1 lb) potatoes,
  sliced

1 Preheat the oven to moderate 180°C (350°F/Gas 4). Cut small deep slits in the lamb and push a piece of garlic into each slit. Combine the oil, rosemary, salt and pepper, and rub the mixture over the lamb using your fingertips.
2 Arrange the tomato halves in the base of a baking dish. Top with the potato slices and place the lamb gently on top. Roast for 1 hour, turning the lamb once. Reduce the oven temperature to warm 160°C (315°F/Gas 2–3), and bake for 10 minutes for medium, or 25 minutes for well done.
3 Remove the lamb, wrap tightly in aluminium foil and leave for 15 minutes before carving. The tomatoes and potatoes can be returned to the oven and cooked for a few more minutes, while the meat is standing, to crisp the potatoes. (If the tomatoes are sticking to the baking dish, sprinkle them with a little water to moisten.)

NUTRITION PER SERVE (6)
*Protein 60 g; Fat 15 g;
Carbohydrate 15 g; Dietary
Fibre 3 g; Cholesterol
165 mg; 1800 kJ (430 cal)*

*Brussels Sprout Gratin (top)
and Herbed Lamb Roast*

Potato and Herb Mash

Preparation time:
  10 minutes
Total cooking time:
  15 minutes
Serves 4

4 large potatoes,
  quartered
1/4 cup (60 ml/2 fl oz)
  milk
40 g (1 1/4 oz) butter
1 tablespoon chopped
  fresh chives
1 tablespoon chopped
  fresh thyme
1 tablespoon chopped
  fresh oregano
1 tablespoon chopped
  fresh marjoram

1 Add the potato to a large pan of boiling salted water. Cook until just tender, then drain.
2 Return the potato to the pan over low heat, add the milk and quickly mash, adding a little more milk if necessary to make the potato a fluffy consistency. Beat in the butter. Stir in the herbs, and season with salt and black pepper. Serve immediately.

NUTRITION PER SERVE
*Protein 7 g; Fat 10 g;
Carbohydrate 35 g; Dietary
Fibre 4 g; Cholesterol
30 mg; 1030 kJ (250 cal)*

Steak and Kidney Pie

Preparation time:
  20 minutes
Total cooking time:
  1 hour 50 minutes
Serves 6

4 lamb kidneys
750 g (1 1/2 lb) round
  steak, cut into cubes
2 tablespoons plain
  flour
1 tablespoon oil
1 onion, chopped
30 g (1 oz) butter
1 tablespoon
  Worcestershire sauce
1 tablespoon tomato
  paste
1/2 cup (125 ml/4 fl oz)
  red wine
1 cup (250 ml/8 fl oz)
  beef stock
1/3 cup (20 g/3/4 oz)
  chopped fresh parsley
1/2 teaspoon dried
  thyme
125 g (4 oz) button
  mushrooms, sliced
375 g (12 oz) frozen
  block puff pastry,
  thawed
1 egg, lightly beaten

1 Peel the skin from the kidneys, cut into quarters and trim any fat or sinew. Toss the meat and kidneys in the flour until well coated. Shake off the excess.
2 Heat the oil in a heavy-based pan and cook the onion for 5 minutes, or until soft. Remove with a slotted spoon. Add the butter to the pan. Brown the meat and kidneys in batches, then return to the pan with the onion.
3 Add the Worcestershire sauce, tomato paste, wine, stock, herbs and mushrooms. Bring to the boil, reduce the heat, cover and simmer for 1 hour, or until the meat is tender. Season with salt and pepper. Allow to cool. Spoon into a 1.5 litre pie dish.
4 Preheat the oven to hot 210°C (415°F/ Gas 6–7). Roll the puff pastry out on a lightly floured surface to 4 cm (1 1/2 inches) larger than the dish. Cut 2 strips from the pastry to fit the rim of the dish. Brush the rim with the beaten egg and press the strips firmly in place. Brush with a little more egg. Place the pastry on top of the pie, pressing the edges together to seal. Trim the edges and cut 2 slits in the top for the steam to escape. Decorate with pastry scraps and brush with egg. Bake for 35–40 minutes, or until golden brown.

NUTRITION PER SERVE
*Protein 35 g; Fat 15 g;
Carbohydrate 5 g; Dietary
Fibre 1 g; Cholesterol
240 mg; 1285 kJ (305 cal)*

*Potato and Herb Mash (top)
with Steak and Kidney Pie*

Risotto Parmesan

Preparation time:
  20 minutes
Total cooking time:
  40 minutes
Serves 4–6

1 litre chicken stock
60 g (2 oz) butter
2 tablespoons olive oil
1 small onion, diced
*1/4 teaspoon saffron
  threads or powder*
250 g (8 oz) arborio rice
*1/2 cup (50 g/1³/4 oz)
  grated Parmesan*
2 tablespoons finely
  chopped fresh parsley

1 Put the stock in a pan
and keep at simmering
point. Heat the butter
and oil in a heavy-
based pan. Add the
onion and saffron.
Cook, stirring, for
2–3 minutes. Add the
rice and stir for
1–2 minutes, or until
the rice is well coated.
2 Add 1/2 cup (125 ml/
4 fl oz) of the stock and
stir over low heat until
it is absorbed. Continue
adding 1/2 cup of stock,
stirring constantly, until
the rice is tender and all
the stock is absorbed
(25–30 minutes). Stir in
the Parmesan and
parsley. Serve at once.

NUTRITION PER SERVE (6)
*Protein 5 g; Fat 20 g;
Carbohydrate 15 g; Dietary
Fibre 1 g; Cholesterol
35 mg; 940 kJ (225 cal)*

Roast Vegetable and Lentil Bake

Preparation time:
  30 minutes
  + 30 minutes soaking
Total cooking time:
  2 hours
Serves 4–6

*1/2 cup (125 g/4 oz) red
  lentils*
2 tablespoons olive oil
1 onion, chopped
2 cloves garlic, crushed
*1/2 teaspoon dried
  oregano*
2 tablespoons tomato
  paste
425 g (14 oz) can
  chopped tomatoes
2 zucchini, sliced
500 g (1 lb) orange
  sweet potato, cubed
500 g (1 lb) pumpkin,
  cubed
1 red capsicum, cubed
50 g (1³/4 oz) butter
50 g (1³/4 oz) plain
  flour
2¹/2 cups (600 ml/
  20 fl oz) milk
*1/4 teaspoon ground
  nutmeg*
1 egg, lightly beaten
1 cup (100 g/3¹/2 oz)
  grated Parmesan

1 Soak the lentils in
1 litre of boiling water
for 30 minutes, then
drain. Heat half the oil
in a large pan and cook
the onion and garlic for
2–3 minutes, or until
soft. Add the lentils,
oregano, tomato paste,
tomatoes and 3 cups
(750 ml/24 fl oz) water.
Simmer, stirring often,
for 1 hour, or until the
lentils are cooked.
2 Meanwhile, preheat
the oven to moderate
180°C (350°F/Gas 4).
Put the vegetables in a
large baking dish. Add
the remaining oil and
toss to coat. Bake for
50 minutes, or until
tender, turning twice.
3 Melt the butter in a
pan. Add the flour and
stir for 1 minute.
Remove from the heat
and whisk in the milk
and nutmeg until
smooth. Return to the
heat, whisk until thick,
then cook over medium
heat for 2 minutes.
Cool slightly, then beat
in the egg and a third
of the Parmesan.
4 Grease a 2.5 litre
ovenproof dish. Spread
the vegetables in the
dish, spoon the lentil
mixture over the top,
then pour in the sauce.
Sprinkle with the
remaining Parmesan.
Bake for 40 minutes, or
until the top is set and
golden brown.

NUTRITION PER SERVE (6)
*Protein 20 g; Fat 20 g;
Carbohydrate 70 g; Dietary
Fibre 9 g; Cholesterol
70 mg; 2300 kJ (530 cal)*

*Roast Vegetable and Lentil Bake (top)
with Risotto Parmesan*

Marinated Rump

Preparation time:
  15 minutes
  + 8 hours marinating
Total cooking time:
  20 minutes
Serves 4–6

*1 kg (2 lb) piece rump
  steak, about 3 cm
  (1 1/2 inches) thick
1 cup (250 ml/8 fl oz)
  dry red wine
1 teaspoon finely
  grated orange rind
1/2 cup (125 ml/4 fl oz)
  orange juice
4 spring onions, sliced
1/3 cup (80 ml/
  2 3/4 fl oz) olive oil
1 tablespoon balsamic
  vinegar
2 cloves garlic, crushed
1 tablespoon olive oil,
  extra*

1 Trim the steak of excess fat. Place the wine, orange rind and juice, spring onion, oil, vinegar and garlic in a large shallow glass or ceramic dish, and mix to combine. Season with salt and pepper. Add the steak and toss to coat. Cover and refrigerate for 8 hours, turning occasionally.
2 Preheat the grill, chargrill pan or the barbecue. Drain the meat well and pat dry with paper towels. Brush lightly with the extra oil and cook over high heat for about 10 minutes each side.
3 Transfer to a warm plate, cover with foil and set aside for 3–4 minutes before carving across the grain into thin slices. Serve immediately with creamy mashed potato or parsnip.

NUTRITION PER SERVE (6)
*Protein 40 g; Fat 20 g;
Carbohydrate 3 g; Dietary
Fibre 0 g; Cholesterol
110 mg; 1600 kJ (380 cal)*

Potato Cubes with Ratatouille

Preparation time:
  25 minutes
Total cooking time:
  1 hour
Serves 4–6

*1 large yellow
  capsicum
1/4 cup (60 ml/2 fl oz)
  olive oil
2 red onions, thinly
  sliced
2–3 cloves garlic, finely
  chopped
1 celery stick, cut into
  thin, 5 cm (2 inch)
  strips
400 g (13 oz) can
  peeled tomatoes,
  chopped and juice
  reserved
4 new potatoes, cut
  into 2.5 cm (1 inch)
  cubes
1 teaspoon fresh thyme
  leaves, optional*

1 Remove the seeds and white membrane from the capsicum, then cut the flesh into strips 5 cm (2 inches) long and 2 cm (3/4 inch) thick. Heat the oil in a large heavy-based frying pan, add the onion and garlic, and cook for 3–4 minutes, or until the onion is softened, but not browned. Add the capsicum and celery, and cook, stirring occasionally, for a further 2–3 minutes.
2 Add the chopped tomatoes with their juice and 1/2 cup (125 ml/4 fl oz) water. Boil for 10 minutes, stirring frequently. The mixture will become reduced and sauce-like, but should not be dry. Stir in the potato cubes. Reduce the heat and simmer, covered, for 30 minutes, or until the potato is cooked. Stir occasionally during cooking. Season with salt and freshly ground black pepper, stir in the thyme leaves (if using), and serve.

NUTRITION PER SERVE (6)
*Protein 5 g; Fat 10 g;
Carbohydrate 20 g; Dietary
Fibre 4 g; Cholesterol
0 mg; 760 kJ (180 cal)*

*Potato Cubes with Ratatouille (top)
and Marinated Rump*

Vegetable Pies

Preparation time:
 1 hour
Total cooking time:
 45 minutes
Makes 6

1 tablespoon oil
1 large onion, chopped
2 cloves garlic, crushed
2 teaspoons ground
 coriander
2 teaspoons ground
 cumin
2 potatoes, chopped
2 zucchini, chopped
1 carrot, chopped
1 parsnip, chopped
350 g (11 oz) pumpkin,
 chopped
3/4 cup (185 ml/6 fl oz)
 chicken stock
6 sheets frozen puff
 pastry, thawed
1 egg, lightly beaten

1 Heat the oil in a large pan and add the onion. Cook over medium heat for 10 minutes, or until very soft and golden, stirring occasionally. Add the garlic, coriander and cumin, and cook, stirring, for 1 minute.
2 Add the vegetables to the pan and stir to combine with the onion mixture. Add the stock and bring to the boil. Reduce the heat to medium-low and cook, partially covered, until the vegetables are tender but not mushy, and the liquid has evaporated. Stir the mixture occasionally. Remove from the pan and cool completely.
3 Preheat the oven to hot 210°C (415°F/ Gas 6–7). Brush a large 6-hole muffin tin with oil. Cut a 17 cm (6 3/4 inch) round from 1 of the pastry sheets. Cut 2 deep 'V's 2 cm (3/4 inch) wide almost to the centre, opposite each other. Fit the pastry into the tin, and fill with the vegetable mixture. Repeat with the remaining pastry and filling.
4 Using the leftover pastry, cut strips 1.5 cm (5/8 inch) wide, long enough to cross each pie. Brush the edge of one of the pies with egg and lay the strips, slightly overlapping, to cover one half of the pie. Gently press the edges to seal, trim the excess pastry, and repeat with the other half of the lid. Brush with the egg, then repeat with the remaining pies and pastry. Bake for 20 minutes, or until the tops are puffed and golden brown. Leave in the tin for a few minutes before easing out with a knife.

NUTRITION PER PIE
Protein 15 g; Fat 40 g; Carbohydrate 70 g; Dietary Fibre 6 g; Cholesterol 70 mg; 2840 kJ (680 cal)

Vegetable Pies

Cook the onion until soft and golden, then add the garlic, coriander and cumin.

Add the stock to the combined vegetables and onion mixture.

Cut 2 deep 'V's in the pastry round, then fit it into the tin.

Overlap the strips of pastry to cover one half of the pie, then trim and repeat.

Potato and Mushroom Gratin

Preparation time:
  15 minutes
Total cooking time:
  1 hour
Serves 4

250 g (8 oz)
  *mushrooms, thickly
  sliced*
150 g (5 oz) soft blue
  *cheese (gorgonzola,
  blue castello or
  dolcelatte)*
650 g (1 lb 5 oz)
  potatoes, thinly sliced
30 g (1 oz) butter,
  melted

1 Preheat the oven to
moderately hot 200°C
(400°F/Gas 6). Layer
half the mushrooms in
a shallow 1.5 litre
ovenproof dish.
Crumble half the cheese
over the mushrooms,
and layer half the
potato on top.
2 Repeat with the
remaining ingredients,
overlapping the potato
on the top. Brush with
the butter and bake for
50–60 minutes, or
until crisp and brown.
Serve immediately.

NUTRITION PER SERVE
*Protein 15 g; Fat 20 g;
Carbohydrate 20 g; Dietary
Fibre 4 g; Cholesterol
60 mg; 1315 kJ (315 cal)*

Veal Cutlets with Caramelized Onions and Leeks

Preparation time:
  35 minutes
Total cooking time:
  1¼ hours
Serves 6

¹/3 cup (80 ml/
  2³/4 fl oz) olive oil
1 kg (2 lb) brown
  onions, thinly sliced
4 leeks, white part only,
  thinly sliced
1 tablespoon brown
  sugar
2 fresh bay leaves or
  1 dried leaf, torn in
  half
6 large veal cutlets,
  trimmed
2 cloves garlic, finely
  chopped
¹/2 teaspoon salt
¹/2 teaspoon freshly
  ground black pepper
2 tablespoons balsamic
  vinegar
3 teaspoons fresh
  lemon thyme leaves
¹/3 cup (80 ml/
  2³/4 fl oz) orange juice
*fresh lemon thyme
sprigs, to garnish*

1 Heat half the olive oil
in a large heavy-based
pan over medium-low
heat. Add the onion
and leek, and cook
slowly for 20 minutes,
stirring occasionally.
Add the brown sugar
and bay leaves, and
cook for a further
20–30 minutes, or until
the mixture is a deep
golden brown. Do not
allow the mixture to
burn—it must be
cooked slowly and
gently to achieve the
caramelized flavour
and colour. Discard the
bay leaves.
2 Combine the cutlets,
garlic, salt and pepper
with the remaining oil,
mixing well to coat.
Heat a large heavy-
based frying pan over
medium heat. Cook the
cutlets for 3 minutes on
each side. Add the
balsamic vinegar and
lemon thyme. Reduce
the heat, cover and
cook for 3 minutes.
Remove the cutlets and
cover with foil. Increase
the heat to high, add
the orange juice and
bring to the boil,
stirring. Set aside.
3 Gently reheat the
onion mixture and
place a heaped serving
on each plate. Place a
veal cutlet on top and
drizzle with the orange
juice mixture. Garnish
with the thyme sprigs,
and serve immediately
with mashed potato
and steamed vegetables.

NUTRITION PER SERVE
*Protein 20 g; Fat 20 g;
Carbohydrate 20 g; Dietary
Fibre 7 g; Cholesterol
60 mg; 1490 kJ (355 cal)*

*Potato and Mushroom Gratin (top) and
Veal Cutlets with Caramelized Onions and Leeks*

Pumpkin and Goats' Cheese Lasagne

Preparation time:
45 minutes
+ 15 minutes standing
Total cooking time:
2 hours 15 minutes
Serves 4–6

1.2 kg (2 lb 6 oz)
  *butternut pumpkin,
  cut into small
  pieces*
1/4 cup (60 ml/2 fl oz)
  olive oil
40 g (1 1/4 oz) butter
1 large onion, finely
  chopped
300 g (10 oz) zucchini,
  grated
2 tablespoons chopped
  fresh parsley
1 tablespoon chopped
  fresh sage
1/4 teaspoon ground
  nutmeg
12 instant lasagne
  sheets
250 g (8 oz) goats'
  *cheese, crumbled
  or thinly sliced
  (see Note)*
1 1/3 cups (200 g/6 1/2 oz)
  *grated mozzarella
  cheese*
30 g (1 oz) butter,
  extra

Béchamel Sauce
40 g (1 1/4 oz) butter
2 tablespoons plain
  flour
2 1/2 cups (600 ml/
  20 fl oz) milk

1 Preheat the oven to moderate 180°C (350°F/Gas 4) and grease a 2.5 litre ovenproof dish. Place the pumpkin on a baking tray and brush with the oil. Bake for 45–55 minutes, or until the pumpkin is tender on the inside and crisp on the outside, turning occasionally.
2 Meanwhile, heat the butter in a pan. When it is foaming, add the chopped onion and cook over low heat for 15 minutes. Add the zucchini, parsley and sage, and cook, covered, for 5 minutes. Set aside.
3 To make the sauce, melt the butter in a pan over medium heat. Add the flour and cook, stirring, for 1 minute. Remove from the heat and stir in the milk. Return to the heat and stir constantly until the sauce boils and thickens. Simmer for 1 minute. Cover the surface of the sauce with baking paper to prevent a skin forming. Leave the sauce to cool.
4 Place the pumpkin and any juice or oil in a food processor with the nutmeg and some salt and pepper. Process until roughly chopped.
5 Spread a very thin layer of béchamel sauce over the bottom of the dish, and arrange a layer of lasagne sheets over the top. Spoon in half of the pumpkin mixture and gently spread it evenly over the lasagne sheets. Spoon in half of the zucchini mixture and drizzle with a little of the béchamel. Scatter a third of the goats' cheese over the top. Repeat with another layer of the lasagne sheets, pumpkin, zucchini, goats' cheese and a little more of the béchamel sauce. Finally, top with the remaining lasagne sheets and béchamel sauce. Scatter with the mozzarella cheese and dot with small pieces of the butter and remaining goats' cheese. Sprinkle with salt and black pepper, and bake for 40–50 minutes, or until the top is golden brown and bubbling. Leave for 15 minutes, then serve.

NUTRITION PER SERVE (6)
*Protein 30 g; Fat 50 g;
Carbohydrate 40 g; Dietary
Fibre 5 g; Cholesterol
115 mg; 3070 kJ (730 cal)*

Note: The texture of goats' cheese varies dramatically depending on the brand—some will crumble, while others can be cut into paper-thin slices.

Pumpkin and Goats' Cheese Lasagne

Soy and Ginger Artichokes

Preparation time:
  10 minutes
Total cooking time:
  50 minutes
Serves 4

500 g (1 lb) Jerusalem
  artichokes, unpeeled
1/3 cup (80 ml/2³/4 fl oz)
  orange juice
2 tablespoons oil
2 tablespoons soy sauce
1 tablespoon honey,
  warmed
2 teaspoons finely
  grated fresh ginger
1 clove garlic, crushed

1 Preheat the oven to
moderate 180°C
(350°F/Gas 4). Scrub
the artichokes well and
pat dry on paper
towels. Prick lightly
with a fine skewer and
add to a pan of boiling
water. Return to the
boil, then simmer for
10 minutes. Drain and
place in a baking dish
in a single layer.
2 Put the remaining
ingredients in a small
bowl, and mix to
combine. Pour the
mixture over the
artichokes and toss well
to coat completely.
3 Bake for 40 minutes,
or until the artichokes
are tender and slightly

caramelized, basting
with the soy mixture
occasionally. Serve the
artichokes with beef,
fish or lamb.

NUTRITION PER SERVE
*Protein 4 g; Fat 10 g;
Carbohydrate 10 g; Dietary
Fibre 1 g; Cholesterol
0 mg; 600 kJ (140 cal)*

Italian Beef

Preparation time:
  10 minutes
Total cooking time:
  45 minutes–1¹/4 hours
Serves 6–8

1.5 kg (3 lb) beef
  Scotch fillet, at room
  temperature
250 g (8 oz) packet
  frozen chopped
  spinach, thawed
1 egg
75 g (2¹/2 oz) pancetta,
  chopped (see Note)
1/3 cup (35 g/1¹/4 oz)
  grated Parmesan
2 tablespoons chopped
  fresh flat-leaf parsley
1 clove garlic, crushed
2 tablespoons olive oil

1 Preheat the oven to
moderately hot 200°C
(400°F/Gas 6).
Butterfly the beef by
cutting it through
lengthways to open
out, without cutting
right through. Remove
any excess fat and

sinew from the meat.
Open the meat out and
flatten it slightly with
the palm of your hand.
2 Squeeze the liquid
from the thawed
spinach. Beat the egg in
a large bowl and add
the spinach, pancetta,
Parmesan, parsley and
garlic. Season the
mixture well with salt
and black pepper, and
spread it evenly over
the beef. Re-shape the
meat and tie it together
with kitchen string at
regular intervals.
3 Heat the oil in a large
heavy-based baking
dish on the stove top,
add the meat and
brown over high heat
on all sides for
5–10 minutes. Place in
the oven and bake for
40 minutes for medium
rare, 50 minutes for
medium or 1 hour for
well done.
4 Transfer the meat to a
large heated plate,
cover loosely with
aluminium foil and
leave in a warm place
for 10 minutes.
Remove the string and
carve the meat into
thick slices to serve.

NUTRITION PER SERVE (8)
*Protein 45 g; Fat 20 g;
Carbohydrate 0 g; Dietary
Fibre 2 g; Cholesterol
195 mg; 1560 kJ (370 cal)*

Note: You may use
prosciutto in place of
the pancetta in this
recipe, if you wish.

*Soy and Ginger Artichokes (top)
with Italian Beef*

Cabbage Rolls

Preparation time:
1 hour
+ 10 minutes soaking
Total cooking time:
55 minutes
Serves 4

8 large savoy cabbage
  leaves
2 tablespoons oil
125 g (4 oz) bacon,
  chopped
2 cloves garlic,
  chopped
1 large onion, finely
  chopped
200 g (6¹/2 oz) pork
  and veal mince
1¹/2 cups (280 g/9 oz)
  cooked short-grain
  white rice
2 small tomatoes, finely
  chopped
2 cups (500 g/1 lb)
  tomato pasta sauce
100 g (3¹/2 oz) sun-
  dried tomatoes, cut
  into thin strips
2 tablespoons chopped
  fresh parsley

1 Place the cabbage leaves in a large bowl and cover with boiling water. Leave for 5 minutes, then remove the leaves and refresh in a large bowl of iced water. Leave for 5 minutes. Drain and pat dry. Cut out the thick section from the stem of the larger, firmer leaves to make them easier to roll.
2 Heat the oil in a frying pan over medium heat. Add the bacon, garlic and onion, and cook for 10 minutes, stirring regularly. Transfer the mixture to a large mixing bowl and combine with the mince, rice and tomato. Season well with salt and pepper, and mix to combine.
3 Place the cabbage leaves on a chopping board with the underside of the leaves facing up. Divide the filling among the leaves, placing it in the centre of each leaf. Carefully fold in the edges and roll each leaf up firmly. Tie a piece of kitchen string around each cabbage roll to prevent it from falling apart.
4 Place the cabbage rolls, seam-side-down, in a deep frying pan. Pour in the pasta sauce and sprinkle with the sun-dried tomato. Cover and bring to the boil, then reduce the heat to a gentle simmer. Cook, covered, for 25 minutes, then uncover and cook for a further 5–10 minutes, or until the sauce is thick. Leave to stand for 5 minutes, then remove the string and scatter with the parsley.

NUTRITION PER SERVE
*Protein 25 g; Fat 25 g;
Carbohydrate 40 g; Dietary
Fibre 7 g; Cholesterol
55 mg; 1865 kJ (445 cal)*

Cabbage Rolls

Refresh the cabbage leaves in a large
bowl of iced water.

Combine the bacon mixture with the
mince, rice and tomato.

Roll the leaves up firmly, then tie with a piece of kitchen string.

Pour in the pasta sauce and sprinkle with the strips of sun-dried tomato.

Chickpea and Vegetable Curry

Preparation time:
20 minutes
Total cooking time:
30 minutes
Serves 4–6

1 tablespoon oil
1 onion, thinly sliced
2–3 cloves garlic, finely
  chopped
1 tablespoon grated
  fresh ginger
1 tablespoon sweet
  chilli sauce
1 teaspoon ground
  turmeric
1 teaspoon ground
  cumin
1/2 teaspoon ground
  coriander
1/2 teaspoon garam
  masala
1 red capsicum, thickly
  sliced
2 zucchini, cut into
  thick strips
1 carrot, cut into thick
  strips
1 celery stick, cut into
  thick strips
100 g (3 1/2 oz) button
  mushrooms, halved
150 g (5 oz) broccoli,
  cut into small florets
300 g (10 oz) can
  chickpeas, drained
400 ml (13 fl oz) can
  coconut milk
1/2 cup (25 g/3/4 oz)
  chopped fresh
  coriander

1 Heat the oil in a large pan, and cook the onion and garlic for 2–3 minutes, or until soft, but not browned. Add the ginger, chilli sauce and spices. Stir for 1–2 minutes.
2 Add the vegetables all at once and stir to coat. Stir in the chickpeas and coconut milk, and bring to the boil. Reduce the heat and simmer, covered, for 15–20 minutes, or until the vegetables are just tender. Stir in the coriander and serve with steamed rice.

NUTRITION PER SERVE (6) *Protein 25 g; Fat 25 g; Carbohydrate 50 g; Dietary Fibre 20 g; Cholesterol 0 mg; 2040 kJ (490 cal)*

Tomato and Fennel in Roasted Red Capsicums

Preparation time:
  20 minutes
Total cooking time:
  1 hour
Serves 6

3 large red capsicums
2 small fennel bulbs
6 Roma tomatoes
6 cloves garlic, sliced
3 teaspoons fennel seeds
juice of 1 lemon
2 tablespoons olive oil

1 Preheat the oven to moderate 180°C (350°F/Gas 4). Brush a large baking dish with oil. Cut the capsicums in half lengthways, leaving the stalk attached. Remove the seeds and membrane.
2 Halve the fennel bulbs and cut into thick slices. Place in a pan of boiling salted water and cook for 1 minute, then drain and cool. Halve the tomatoes lengthways, and arrange with the fennel slices in the capsicum halves. (The amount of fennel used will depend on the size of the capsicums and the fennel, but the vegetables should fit firmly inside the capsicum halves.) Add the garlic slices to each capsicum half and sprinkle with the fennel seeds. Season with salt and freshly ground black pepper. Sprinkle the lemon juice and half the oil over the capsicums and brush with the remaining olive oil.
3 Bake for 1 hour, or until the capsicums are tender, brushing lightly with the oil once or twice during cooking. Serve hot.

NUTRITION PER SERVE *Protein 3 g; Fat 7 g; Carbohydrate 9 g; Dietary Fibre 4 g; Cholesterol 0 mg; 470 kJ (115 cal)*

Tomato and Fennel in Roasted Red Capsicums (top) with Chickpea and Vegetable Curry

Traditional Corned Beef and Vegetables

Preparation time:
  25 minutes
  + 1 hour soaking
Total cooking time:
  2 hours
Serves 4

1.2 kg (2 lb 6 oz)
  corned silverside (beef)
10 *whole cloves*
1 *onion*
8 *black peppercorns*
2 *bay leaves*
2 *tablespoons brown*
  sugar
4 *carrots*
4 *potatoes*
1/4 large cabbage

Parsley Sauce
40 g (1*1/4 oz) butter*
2 *tablespoons plain*
  flour
2 *cups (500 ml/16 fl.oz)*
  milk
2 *tablespoons chopped*
  fresh parsley

1 Soak the beef in cold water for 1 hour, changing the water 3 times. Remove the beef from the water and pat dry. Using a sharp knife, cut a diamond pattern into the white layer of fat. Press the cloves into the flesh of the onion.
2 Place the beef in a large heavy-based pan. Add enough water to just cover the beef, and add the clove-studded onion, peppercorns, bay leaves and brown sugar. Cover and bring the water to a gentle simmer. Cook for about 1¹/₂ hours, spooning the cooking liquid over the top of the meat occasionally. Do not allow the water to boil or the meat will become tough. While the beef is cooking, make the parsley sauce.
3 To make the parsley sauce, melt the butter in a pan over medium heat. When the butter is foaming, stir in the flour and cook, stirring, for 1 minute. Remove from the heat and add the milk, stirring constantly until the sauce is smooth. Return the pan to the heat and cook, stirring constantly, until the sauce boils and thickens. Boil for 1 minute further. Season well with salt and freshly ground black pepper. Cover the surface of the sauce with baking paper to prevent a skin forming. Set aside.
4 When the meat is cooked and tender, remove it from the pan, wrap in aluminium foil and set aside for 15 minutes while cooking the vegetables.

Halve the carrots and potatoes and add to the pan that the beef was cooked in. Simmer for about 10 minutes, then add the wedge of cabbage and cook for about 4 minutes. Test all the vegetables with a sharp knife for tenderness; when they are cooked, remove them from the pan and set aside. Reserve about 1/2 cup (125 ml/4 fl oz) of the cooking liquid to add to the sauce.
5 To serve, remove the paper from the sauce, stir in the reserved cooking liquid and parsley, and stir over low heat until the sauce is heated through. Slice the meat into thick slices and arrange on a large warmed serving platter. Slice the cabbage, and arrange the vegetables around the meat. Spoon about a third of the parsley sauce over the sliced beef. Serve immediately, with the remaining parsley sauce in a jug.

NUTRITION PER SERVE
Protein 60 g; Fat 20 g; Carbohydrate 50 g; Dietary Fibre 9 g; Cholesterol 180 mg; 2615 kJ (625 cal)

Note: Be sure to soak the beef and change the water before cooking, or the cooked beef will be extremely salty.

Traditional Corned Beef and Vegetables

Spiced Red Cabbage

Preparation time:
20 minutes
Total cooking time:
1 1/2 hours
Serves 4–6

750 g (1 1/2 lb) red
 cabbage
1 large red onion,
 chopped
1 green apple, cored
 and chopped
2 cloves garlic, crushed
1/4 teaspoon ground
 cloves
1/4 teaspoon ground
 nutmeg
1 1/2 tablespoons brown
 sugar
2 tablespoons red wine
 vinegar
20 g (3/4 oz) butter,
 cubed

1 Preheat the oven to
slow 150°C (300°F/
Gas 2). Quarter the
cabbage and remove
the core. Finely slice the
cabbage and put it in a
large casserole dish
with the onion and
apple. Toss well.
2 Combine the garlic,
spices, sugar and
vinegar in a small bowl.
Pour the mixture over
the cabbage, and toss
to combine. Dot the
top with the butter.
Cover and bake for

1 1/2 hours, stirring
once or twice. Season
to taste with salt and
freshly ground black
pepper, and serve hot.

NUTRITION PER SERVE (6)
*Protein 3 g; Fat 3 g;
Carbohydrate 10 g; Dietary
Fibre 6 g; Cholesterol
9 mg; 370 kJ (90 cal)*

Pork Chops in Normandy Sauce

Preparation time:
 25 minutes
Total cooking time:
 55 minutes
Serves 4

40 g (1 1/4 oz) butter
12 French shallots
2 cloves garlic, chopped
4 thick pork chops,
 trimmed of fat
1 1/2 cups (375 ml/
 12 fl oz) apple cider
1 tablespoon white
 wine vinegar
3 teaspoons French
 mustard
1 green apple, cored
 and cut into 8 slices
2 teaspoons brown
 sugar
1/4 cup (60 ml/2 fl oz)
 cream
2 teaspoons cornflour
small fresh thyme
 sprigs, to garnish

1 Heat half the butter
in a large heavy-based
frying pan. Add the

shallots and garlic, and
cook for 3–4 minutes,
or until soft. Remove
and set aside. Add the
chops to the pan. Cook
over high heat, turning
once, for 2–3 minutes,
or until browned.
2 Reduce the heat and
return the shallots and
garlic to the pan. Pour
in the combined cider,
vinegar and mustard.
Cover and simmer for
about 20 minutes, or
until the pork chops are
tender. (The cooking
time will depend on the
thickness of the pork.)
3 Meanwhile, heat the
remaining butter in a
small frying pan. Add
the apple slices and
brown sugar. Cook,
turning occasionally,
for 3 minutes, or until
the apple has lightly
browned and softened.
Remove and set aside.
4 Remove the pork
chops from the pan,
cover with foil and
keep warm. Combine
the cream and
cornflour, then add to
the cider mixture.
Whisk quickly for
5–10 minutes, or until
the sauce has thickened
slightly. Add the apple
and pork chops, and
heat through for
5 minutes. Garnish
with the thyme sprigs.

NUTRITION PER SERVE
*Protein 25 g; Fat 20 g;
Carbohydrate 20 g; Dietary
Fibre 1 g; Cholesterol
95 mg; 1350 kJ (320 cal)*

*Spiced Red Cabbage (top)
and Pork Chops in Normandy Sauce*

Steamed Lemon Pudding

Preparation time:
40 minutes
Total cooking time:
1 hour 35 minutes
Serves 8

100 g (3¹/2 oz) butter
¹/2 cup (125 g/4 oz)
  caster sugar
3 eggs, lightly beaten
2 teaspoons finely
  grated lemon rind
1¹/2 cups (185 g/6 oz)
  self-raising flour
¹/4 cup (30 g/1 oz) plain
  flour
2 tablespoons milk

Lemon Curd Cream
¹/4 cup (60 g/2 oz)
  caster sugar
50 g (1³/4 oz) butter
2 teaspoons finely
  grated lemon rind
2 tablespoons lemon
  juice
3 egg yolks
³/4 cup (185 ml/6 fl oz)
  cream

1 Brush a 1.5 litre aluminium pudding basin with melted butter and line the base with baking paper. Brush a sheet of foil with melted butter and lay a sheet of baking paper on the greased side of the foil. Make a pleat along the centre.
2 Using electric beaters, cream the butter and sugar. Beat in the eggs one at a time until combined, then beat in the rind. Fold in the flours and milk until just combined. Transfer to the pudding basin and cover with the foil and paper, foil-side-up.
3 Place the lid over the foil and secure the clips. Place the basin on an upturned saucer in a large, deep pan. Pour boiling water down the side of the pan to come halfway up the basin. Bring to the boil, reduce the heat slightly and simmer, covered, for 1 hour 20 minutes, or until a skewer comes out clean when inserted into the pudding. Add more boiling water to the pan as necessary: do not let it boil dry.
4 To make the lemon curd cream, put the sugar, butter, rind and juice in a heatproof bowl. Stir over a pan of simmering water until the butter has melted and the sugar dissolved. Add the egg yolks and stir constantly for 10 minutes, or until the mixture thickens. Add the cream gradually and stir until heated through.
5 Leave the pudding for 5 minutes before turning out. Cut into wedges and drizzle with the lemon curd cream.

NUTRITION PER SERVE
Protein 7 g; Fat 20 g; Carbohydrate 50 g; Dietary Fibre 1 g; Cholesterol 180 mg; 1005 kJ (385 cal)

Steamed Lemon Pudding

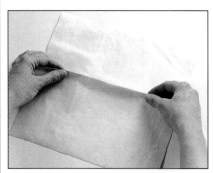

Lay a sheet of baking paper on the foil and make a wide pleat along the centre.

Fold in the flours and milk until just combined, taking care not to overbeat.

Cover the pudding basin with the foil and paper, foil-side-up.

Add the egg yolks and stir constantly until the mixture thickens.

Spicy Rhubarb Crumble

Preparation time:
10 minutes
Total cooking time:
35 minutes
Serves 4

3 green apples, cored
 and cut into small
 pieces
1/4 cup (60 g/2 oz)
 sugar
410 g (13 oz) rhubarb,
 cut into small pieces
1 tablespoon finely
 chopped glacé ginger

Topping
1 cup (130 g/4 1/4 oz)
 natural muesli
60 g (2 oz) butter,
 melted
1/3 cup (75 g/2 1/2 oz)
 demerara sugar
1/2 teaspoon ground
 cinnamon
1/4 teaspoon ground
 cloves
1/4 teaspoon ground
 nutmeg

1 Preheat the oven to
moderate 180°C
(350°F/Gas 4), and
lightly grease a shallow
20 cm (8 inch) square
ovenproof dish. Place
the apple in a pan with
the sugar and 1/2 cup
(125 ml/4 fl oz) water.
Slowly bring to the
boil, stirring to dissolve
the sugar. Reduce the
heat and simmer for
5 minutes. Add the
rhubarb and ginger,
cover and cook for
5 minutes, or until the
apple is soft. Spoon
into the dish.
2 To make the topping,
combine the ingredients
in a bowl. Stir until
crumbly and the butter
is evenly distributed.
3 Sprinkle the topping
over the fruit. Bake for
15–20 minutes, or until
the topping is golden
and crisp. Serve with
cream or ice cream.

NUTRITION PER SERVE
*Protein 5 g; Fat 15 g;
Carbohydrate 70 g; Dietary
Fibre 8 g; Cholesterol
40 mg; 1805 kJ (430 cal)*

Rice Pudding

Preparation time:
 15 minutes
 + 10 minutes draining
Total cooking time:
 1 hour 45 minutes
Serves 4–6

1/2 cup (110 g/3 1/2 oz)
 short-grain white rice
1 litre milk
1 teaspoon grated
 lemon rind
2/3 cup (170 ml/
 5 1/2 fl oz) cream
3 eggs, separated
2–3 tablespoons caster
 sugar

1 Preheat the oven to
warm 160°C (315°F/
Gas 2–3). Grease a
1.75 litre ovenproof
dish with butter. Half
fill a baking dish with
water and place in the
oven. Wash the rice and
leave it to drain in a
sieve for 10 minutes.
2 Bring 2/3 cup (170 ml/
5 1/2 fl oz) water to the
boil in a heavy-based
pan, stir in the rice and
boil for 2 minutes, or
until the water is
absorbed. (Watch the
rice does not stick to
the pan.) Stir in the
milk and lemon rind,
and bring to the boil,
stirring. Reduce the
heat and simmer for
15 minutes, or until the
rice is cooked, stirring
occasionally. Cool for
5 minutes, then whisk
in the cream, egg yolks
and sugar, to taste.
3 Beat the egg whites in
a small bowl until soft
peaks form. Gently fold
into the rice mixture
and pour into the dish.
Place the dish in the
baking dish and bake
for 1 hour, or until just
lightly browned on top.
Cover with foil and
bake for 20 minutes, or
until set. Sprinkle with
sifted icing sugar and
serve warm with
whipped cream.

NUTRITION PER SERVE (6)
*Protein 10 g; Fat 20 g;
Carbohydrate 20 g; Dietary
Fibre 0 g; Cholesterol
150 mg; 1260 kJ (300 cal)*

*Rice Pudding (top)
and Spicy Rhubarb Crumble*

Chocolate, Fig and Pecan Puddings with Hot Chocolate Sauce

Preparation time:
  40 minutes
Total cooking time:
  55 minutes
Serves 4

1/2 cup (50 g/1³/4 oz)
  pecans
1/2 cup (80 g/2³/4 oz)
  dried figs, finely
  chopped
2 cups (160 g/5¹/2 oz)
  fresh breadcrumbs
150 g (5 oz) dark
  chocolate, chopped
1/2 cup (125 ml/4 fl oz)
  milk
60 g (2 oz) butter,
  softened
2 tablespoons caster
  sugar
2 eggs, separated

Hot Chocolate Sauce
60 g (2 oz) dark
  chocolate, chopped
20 g (³/4 oz) butter
1 tablespoon icing
  sugar, sifted
1 teaspoon coffee
  granules
1/4 cup (60 ml/2 fl oz)
  cream

1 Preheat the oven to moderate 180°C (350°F/Gas 4). Lightly grease four 1 cup (250 ml/8 fl oz) moulds and line the bases with baking paper. Brush 4 small sheets of aluminium foil with melted butter or oil. Lay a small sheet of baking paper over the greased side of each piece of foil and make a pleat down the centre.
2 Lightly toast the pecans under a preheated hot grill, then chop them finely. Place in a large bowl with the chopped figs and breadcrumbs.
3 Combine the chocolate and milk in a small pan. Heat gently until the chocolate has melted, then pour the mixture over the pecans, figs and breadcrumbs. Mix together, then set aside to cool. Beat the butter and sugar in a bowl with electric beaters for 2–3 minutes, or until light and creamy, then beat in the egg yolks one at a time. Add this mixture to the cooled breadcrumb mixture and stir until thoroughly combined. Beat the egg whites with electric beaters until soft peaks form. Using a metal spoon, carefully fold the whites through the pudding mixture.
4 Spoon the mixture evenly into the prepared moulds and smooth the surface.

Cover each with a piece of the greased foil and paper, foil-side-up. Tie securely with kitchen string. Place the moulds in a large deep baking dish and carefully pour boiling water down the side of the dish to come halfway up the sides of the moulds. Bake for 45 minutes, or until a skewer comes out clean when inserted into the centre of a pudding. Meanwhile, when the puddings are almost cooked, make the hot chocolate sauce.
5 To make the sauce, combine the chopped chocolate with the butter, icing sugar, coffee granules and cream in a heatproof bowl. Place the bowl over a pan of simmering water and stir constantly for 3–4 minutes, or until the mixture is smooth. Do not overheat.
6 When the puddings are cooked, leave to cool for 5 minutes, then carefully turn out onto individual serving plates. Pour the hot chocolate sauce over the puddings and serve with whipped cream.

NUTRITION PER SERVE
*Protein 15 g; Fat 50 g;
Carbohydrate 85 g; Dietary
Fibre 6 g; Cholesterol
290 mg; 3600 kJ (860 cal)*

*Chocolate, Fig and Pecan Puddings
with Hot Chocolate Sauce*

Poached Pears

Preparation time:
  10 minutes
Total cooking time:
  1 hour 10 minutes
Serves 4

4 large beurre bosc or
  Josephine pears
1¹/2 cups (375 ml/
  12 fl oz) botrytis
  Riesling (see Note)
³/4 cup (185 g/6 oz)
  sugar
1 vanilla pod, split
  lengthways
1 cinnamon stick
mascarpone, to serve

1 Peel the pears,
keeping the stalks
attached. Put 1¹/2 cups
(375 ml/12 fl oz) water
in a large pan with the
wine, sugar, vanilla pod
and cinnamon stick.
Stir over medium heat
until the sugar has
dissolved. Bring to the
boil and simmer for
5 minutes. Stand the
pears upright in the
syrup and, using a
large spoon, gently
spoon a little of the
syrup over the pears to
coat them.
2 Cover and simmer
the pears gently for
30–40 minutes, or until
tender. Test to see if
they are cooked by
piercing with a sharp
knife. Remove the
pears from the pan
with a slotted spoon
and place on warmed
serving plates.
3 Remove and discard
the vanilla pod and
cinnamon stick. Bring
the syrup to the boil,
then boil rapidly for
15 minutes, or until
reduced by half. Pour
the boiled syrup over
the pears and serve
with mascarpone or
thick cream.

NUTRITION PER SERVE
*Protein 0 g; Fat 0 g;
Carbohydrate 70 g; Dietary
Fibre 3 g; Cholesterol
0 mg; 1290 kJ (300 cal)*

Note: Any sweet
dessert wine, such as
Sauternes or Muscat,
can replace the botrytis
Riesling in this recipe.

Golden Syrup Dumplings

Preparation time:
  15 minutes
Total cooking time:
  30 minutes
Serves 4

1 cup (125 g/4 oz) self-
  raising flour
pinch of salt
40 g (1¹/4 oz) butter,
  chopped
1 egg
1 tablespoon milk

Syrup
1 cup (250 g/8 oz)
  sugar
40 g (1¹/4 oz) butter
2 tablespoons golden
  syrup
¹/4 cup (60 ml/2 fl oz)
  lemon juice

1 Sift the flour and salt
into a bowl. Using your
fingertips, rub in the
butter until the mixture
is fine and crumbly, and
make a well in the
centre. Using a flat-
bladed knife, stir the
combined egg and milk
into the flour mixture
to form a soft dough.
2 To make the syrup,
put 2 cups (500 ml/
16 fl oz) water in a
large pan with the
sugar, butter, golden
syrup and lemon juice.
Stir over medium heat
until combined and the
sugar has dissolved.
3 Bring to the boil,
then gently drop
dessertspoons of the
dough into the syrup.
Cover and reduce the
heat to a simmer. Cook
for 20 minutes, or until
a knife inserted into a
dumpling comes out
clean. Spoon onto
serving plates and
drizzle with some of the
syrup. Serve the
dumplings immediately
with whipped cream.

NUTRITION PER SERVE
*Protein 5 g; Fat 20 g;
Carbohydrate 100 g; Dietary
Fibre 1 g; Cholesterol
100 mg; 2330 kJ (560 cal)*

*Golden Syrup Dumplings (top)
and Poached Pears*

Jam Puddings with Vanilla Custard

Preparation time:
30 minutes
Total cooking time:
55 minutes
Serves 6

185 g (6 oz) butter,
  softened
3/4 cup (185 g/6 oz)
  caster sugar
1 teaspoon vanilla
  essence
3 eggs, lightly beaten
1/2 cup (60 g/2 oz)
  plain flour
1 cup (125 g/4 oz) self-
  raising flour
1/2 cup (160 g/5 1/4 oz)
  jam (see Note)

Vanilla Custard
4 egg yolks
1/4 cup (60 g/2 oz)
  caster sugar
1 teaspoon cornflour
1 teaspoon vanilla
  essence
1 1/2 cups (375 ml/
  12 fl oz) milk
1/2 cup (125 ml/4 fl oz)
  cream

1 Preheat the oven to moderate 180°C (350°F/Gas 4). Lightly grease six 1 cup (250 ml/8 fl oz) fluted or plain heatproof moulds. Grease 6 small sheets of aluminium foil with melted butter or oil. Lay a small sheet of baking paper over the greased side of each sheet of foil, and make a pleat along the centre.

2 Beat the butter, sugar and vanilla essence with electric beaters for 1–2 minutes, or until light and creamy. Add the eggs gradually, beating well between each addition. Using a metal spoon, fold in the combined sifted flours, a quarter at a time.

3 Spoon the mixture evenly into the moulds and smooth the surface. Cover each with a piece of greased foil and paper, foil-side-up. Tie securely with kitchen string. Place the moulds in a large deep baking dish. Carefully pour boiling water down the side of the dish to come halfway up the sides of the moulds.

4 Bake for 45 minutes, or until a skewer inserted into the centre of a pudding comes out clean. Meanwhile, when the pudding is almost ready, make the vanilla custard.

5 To make the custard, whisk the egg yolks, sugar, cornflour and vanilla essence for 2 minutes, or until creamy. Place the milk and cream in a pan and heat slowly until the mixture reaches boiling point. Pour the hot mixture over the beaten egg yolks and sugar, beating continuously with a whisk. Return the mixture to the pan and stir over low heat until it has thickened slightly and will coat the back of a metal spoon. Do not allow the mixture to boil or it will curdle.

6 Put the jam in a small pan. Warm gently over low heat for 3–4 minutes, or until it is liquid. Be careful not to let the jam burn.

7 Leave the cooked puddings for 5 minutes before loosening the sides with a knife and turning them out onto individual plates. Serve hot, topped with the warmed jam and surrounded with the hot vanilla custard.

NUTRITION PER SERVE
Protein 15 g; Fat 40 g; Carbohydrate 85 g; Dietary Fibre 2 g; Cholesterol 330 mg; 3180 kJ (760 cal)

Note: Raspberry, mixed berry, plum, apricot or sour cherry jam are all suitable for this recipe. The puddings may be frozen for up to 2 months. Remove from the tins and cool on a wire rack, then wrap them in foil, place in a plastic bag, and freeze. Reheat in a moderate 180°C (350°F/Gas 4) oven for 15–20 minutes.

Jam Puddings with Vanilla Custard

Sticky Date Pudding

Preparation time:
  30 minutes
Total cooking time:
  55 minutes
Serves 6–8

200 g (6¹/2 oz) dates,
  pitted and chopped
1 teaspoon bicarbonate
  of soda
100 g (3¹/2 oz) butter
²/3 cup (160 g/5¹/2 oz)
  caster sugar
2 eggs, lightly beaten
1 teaspoon vanilla
  essence
1¹/2 cups (185 g/6 oz)
  self-raising flour

Sauce
1 cup (230 g/7¹/2 oz)
  firmly packed soft
  brown sugar
¹/2 cup (125 ml/4 fl oz)
  cream
100 g (3¹/2 oz) butter

1 Preheat the oven to moderate 180°C (350°F/Gas 4). Grease a 20 cm (8 inch) square cake tin, and line the base with baking paper. Combine the dates with 1 cup (250 ml/8 fl oz) water in a small pan. Bring to the boil, then remove from the heat. Stir in the bicarbonate of soda and cool to room temperature.

2 Using electric beaters, beat the butter and sugar in a small bowl until it is light and creamy. Add the eggs gradually, beating thoroughly after each addition. Beat in the vanilla essence until combined. Transfer to a large bowl.

3 Using a metal spoon, fold in the flour and the date mixture, and stir until just combined— do not overbeat. Pour into the tin and bake for 50 minutes, or until a skewer comes out clean when inserted into the centre of the pudding. Leave for 10 minutes before turning out. While the pudding is cooking, make the sauce.

4 To make the sauce, combine the sugar, cream and butter in a small pan. Stir until the butter melts and the sugar dissolves. Bring to the boil, reduce the heat and simmer for 2 minutes. Cut the pudding into pieces, drizzle with the hot sauce and serve immediately. Delicious served with thick cream or mascarpone.

NUTRITION PER SERVE (8)
*Protein 5 g; Fat 30 g;
Carbohydrate 60 g; Dietary
Fibre 3 g; Cholesterol
130 mg; 2090 kJ (500 cal)*

Bread and Butter Pudding

Preparation time:
  10 minutes
Total cooking time:
  50 minutes
Serves 4–6

30 g (1 oz) butter,
  softened
6 thin slices day-old
  bread, crusts removed
³/4 cup (140 g/4¹/2 oz)
  mixed dried fruit
¹/4 cup (60 g/2 oz)
  caster sugar
1 teaspoon mixed spice
2 eggs, lightly beaten
1 teaspoon vanilla
  essence
2¹/2 cups (600 ml/
  20 fl oz) milk

1 Preheat the oven to moderate 180°C (350°F/Gas 4). Grease a shallow ovenproof dish. Butter the bread and halve diagonally. Layer the bread in the dish, sprinkling each layer with the fruit, sugar and spice.

2 Beat the eggs, vanilla and milk together. Pour over the bread and leave for 5 minutes. Bake the pudding for 40–50 minutes, or until it is set and the top is browned.

NUTRITION PER SERVE (6)
*Protein 9 g; Fat 10 g;
Carbohydrate 45 g; Dietary
Fibre 2 g; Cholesterol
90 mg; 1260 kJ (300 cal)*

*Bread and Butter Pudding (top)
with Sticky Date Pudding*

Winter Pear Tart

Preparation time:
  20 minutes
  + 1 hour marinating
Total cooking time:
  50 minutes
Serves 4–6

2 large beurre bosc
  pears (about 600 g/
  1¹/4 lb)
75 ml (2¹/2 fl oz) white
  wine
¹/4 cup (60 g/2 oz)
  caster sugar
225 ml (7 fl oz) milk
3 eggs
2 teaspoons vanilla
  essence
75 g (2¹/2 oz) plain
  flour
icing sugar, to sprinkle

1 Peel and core the pears, and cut them into 12 slices each. Place in a large bowl and pour in the combined wine and sugar. Gently stir and set aside for 1 hour. (Do not leave for any longer or the pears will turn brown.)
2 Preheat the oven to moderate 180°C (350°F/Gas 4), and grease a shallow, round 1.25 litre ovenproof dish. Remove the pear slices from the syrup and spread evenly over the base of the dish.
3 Pour the syrup into the bowl of a food processor. With the motor running, add the milk, eggs, vanilla essence and flour. Process until smooth, then pour the mixture over the pears. Bake for 50 minutes, or until the tart is puffed and golden on top. Sprinkle the sifted icing sugar liberally over the top. Serve the tart hot or warm with thick cream or ice cream.

NUTRITION PER SERVE (6)
*Protein 6 g; Fat 4 g;
Carbohydrate 35 g; Dietary
Fibre 3 g; Cholesterol
95 mg; 860 kJ (205 cal)*

Raisin Scones

Preparation time:
  25 minutes
Total cooking time:
  25 minutes
Makes about 12

2¹/4 cups (280 g/9 oz)
  self-raising flour
pinch of salt
1 tablespoon sugar
20 g (³/4 oz) butter,
  chopped
¹/4 cup (50 g/1³/4 oz)
  chopped raisins
1 egg
³/4 cup (185 ml/6 fl oz)
  milk
milk, extra, for glazing

1 Preheat the oven to hot 220°C (425°F/Gas 7). Sift the flour, salt and sugar into a large bowl. Rub in the butter, using your fingertips, until the mixture is fine and crumbly. Stir in the raisins and make a well in the centre.
2 Lightly beat the egg and milk in a small bowl. Add almost all the egg mixture at once to the flour mixture. Mix lightly with a flat-bladed knife to form a soft dough, adding the remaining egg mixture if needed.
3 Gather the dough together and turn it out onto a lightly floured surface. Knead it very lightly for 30 seconds, then press it out to 2.5 cm (1 inch) thick. Cut rounds from the dough using a floured 5 cm (2 inch) cutter.
4 Heat a baking tray in the oven for 5 minutes. Place the rounds on the heated tray, leaving a small gap around each. Brush with the extra milk. Bake for 15–20 minutes, or until the tops are golden brown. Wrap in a clean tea towel while still hot. Serve warm or cold, with butter.

NUTRITION PER SCONE
*Protein 5 g; Fat 4 g;
Carbohydrate 25 g; Dietary
Fibre 1 g; Cholesterol
50 mg; 605 kJ (145 cal)*

*Raisin Scones (top)
and Winter Pear Tart*

Warming Winter Drinks

What better way to pass a cold winter's night than curled up in front of a blazing fire with a steaming, creamy chocolate drink, or a hot, potent nightcap?

Hot Toddy

Put 2 teaspoons brown sugar, 2 slices of lemon, 2 cinnamon sticks, 6 whole cloves, 1/4 cup (60 ml/2 fl oz) whisky and 2 cups (500 ml/ 16 fl oz) boiling water in a heatproof jug. Stir to combine and leave to infuse for a few minutes, then strain through a sieve. Add a little more sugar if necessary. Serves 2

NUTRITION PER SERVE
*Protein 0 g; Fat 0 g;
Carbohydrate 9 g; Dietary
Fibre 0 g; Cholesterol
0 mg; 2180 kJ (520 cal)*

Chocolate Hazelnut Drink

Place 2 cups (500 ml/ 16 fl oz) milk, 1/4 cup (80 g/2³/4 oz) chocolate hazelnut spread and 50 g (1³/4 oz) finely chopped dark chocolate in a pan and heat slowly, without boiling. Stir constantly for 5 minutes, or until the chocolate has melted. Divide between 2 mugs and top with whipped cream and roughly chopped hazelnuts. Serves 2

NUTRITION PER SERVE
*Protein 18 g; Fat 50 g;
Carbohydrate 30 g; Dietary
Fibre 0 g; Cholesterol
50 mg; 3615 kJ (905 cal)*

Hot Buttered Rum

Place 2 teaspoons sugar, 1/2 cup (125 ml/ 4 fl oz) rum and 1 cup (250 ml/8 fl oz) boiling water in a heatproof jug. Stir to dissolve the sugar, then divide between 2 mugs. Stir 1–2 teaspoons unsalted butter into each mug and serve immediately. Serves 2

NUTRITION PER SERVE
*Protein 0 g; Fat 4 g;
Carbohydrate 10 g; Dietary
Fibre 0 g; Cholesterol
10 mg; 850 kJ (200 cal)*

Hot Chocolate

Finely chop 100 g
(6¹/2 oz) dark chocolate
and place in a medium
pan. Add ¹/4 cup
(60 ml/2 fl oz) hot
water, and stir over low
heat until the chocolate
has melted. Gradually
add 1¹/2 cups (375 ml/
12 fl oz) milk and
¹/2 cup (125 ml/4 fl oz)
cream, whisking until
smooth and slightly
frothy, without boiling.
Pour into 2 mugs and
float a couple of
marshmallows on top.
Serves 2

NUTRITION PER SERVE
Protein 10 g; Fat 50 g;
Carbohydrate 40 g; Dietary
Fibre 0 g; Cholesterol
110 mg; 2640 kJ (630 cal)

Hot Caramel and Vanilla Milk Shake

Slowly heat 2 cups
(500 ml/16 fl oz) milk
in a pan. Be careful not
to boil the milk. Add
50 g (1³/4 oz) hard
caramels, such as
Columbines, and heat
until melted, stirring
occasionally. Place in a
blender with
1–2 scoops vanilla ice
cream, and process
briefly until smooth.
Pour the mixture into
2 tall glasses. Serves 2

NUTRITION PER SERVE
Protein 10 g; Fat 15 g;
Carbohydrate 40 g; Dietary
Fibre 0 g; Cholesterol
40 mg; 1390 kJ (330 cal)

Mulled Wine

Stick 12 cloves into
2 oranges, and place in
a small deep pan with
¹/4 cup (45 g/1¹/2 oz)
lightly packed brown
sugar, 1 grated nutmeg,
4 cinnamon sticks and
2 sliced lemons. Add
2 cups (500 ml/16 fl oz)
water, and bring to the
boil. Simmer for
20 minutes, or until the
syrup is fragrant and
infused with the spices.
Remove the spices and
add 3 cups (750 ml/
24 fl oz) full-bodied,
dry red wine. Heat
slowly, without boiling.
Serves 4

NUTRITION PER SERVE
Protein 3 g; Fat 0 g;
Carbohydrate 40 g; Dietary
Fibre 4 g; Cholesterol
0 mg; 1750 kJ (420 cal)

From left: Hot Toddy; Chocolate Hazelnut Drink;
Hot Buttered Rum; Hot Chocolate; Hot Caramel
and Vanilla Milk Shake; Mulled Wine

Index